WITHIN OUR TIME

Edited by

Heather Killingray

First published in Great Britain in 2002 by
POETRY NOW
Remus House,
Coltsfoot Drive,
Peterborough, PE2 9JX
Telephone (01733) 898101
Fax (01733) 313524

HB ISBN 0 75432 780 9
SB ISBN 0 75432 781 7

FOREWORD

Although we are a nation of poets we are accused of not reading poetry, or buying poetry books. After many years of listening to the incessant gripes of poetry publishers, I can only assume that the books they publish, in general, are books that most people do not want to read.

Poetry should not be obscure, introverted, and as cryptic as a crossword puzzle: it is the poet's duty to reach out and embrace the world.

The world owes the poet nothing and we should not be expected to dig and delve into a rambling discourse searching for some inner meaning.

The reason we write poetry (and almost all of us do) is because we want to communicate: an ideal; an idea; or a specific feeling. Poetry is as essential in communication, as a letter; a radio; a telephone, and the main criterion for selecting the poems in this anthology is very simple: they communicate.

Cows in County Durham
on page 116.

Written by
Susan Carole Roberts.

CONTENTS

NO RICH OR POOR

When will human kind unite,
In universal peace,
Deny the constant urge to fight,
And cause all wars to cease,
The way ahead, to me is clear,
If I may dare to judge,
The two main things we have to fear,
Are poverty and grudge,
Let everyone of every cast,
Have food, and room to live,
Tell everyone, forget the past,
And teach them to forgive,
What'er religion you applaud,
Regardless of which sect,
Revere and praise your chosen god,
And show the rest respect,
The world's soldiers heed the call,
To fight where'er they're sent,
The basic urge to fight at all,
Is born of discontent,
World peace can only come to pass,
When we all feel secure,
No lower, and no upper class,
And so, no rich or poor.

Matthew L Burns

CRIME, WAR, LEGALITY

It is against the law
For a loving mate to ease
The pain of his crippled spouse
By ending her physical life with mercy.
It is not against the law
To kill thousands of our fellow creatures,
On whom we depend, because we know not
Why they are dis-eased.
It is not against the law
To kill and maim mothers and children
Of a different race
In the 'legal' crime called war!
No one wants to die
But we are willing for others to be killed
As long as it's not 'us' or 'ours'.
There is no reward or punishment
Or victory or loss
When adversaries kill each other.
How can a thousand dead
Rejoice in victory over
An opposing thousand dead?
A place fit for heroes to live in
Does not exist for those who do not return.
We murdered Christ Jesus
But He proved there is no death.
No wonder He said,
'My kingdom is not of this world!'
'I will arise and go to my father.'
This barren land called Earth
Wallows under the authority of mankind
And Satan, unless we learn to love.

Until we stop completely
The manufacture of munitions -
Guns, missiles, bombs, lethal weapons:
Until we disarm all over the world
And abolish all forms of wasteful
Monetary worship
This kingdom will descend even further
And end in devastation, destruction
In its utter dissolute, deserved demise.
Death brings new life,
Better for those who live love now.
Worse for those who promulgate
And delight in evil in this present state
Where after-life will bring prolonged perdition
And a remorseful, bitter fate!

David W Hill

THE KING OF TERROR

He is the hero of the night -
He would rather hide than fight -
In a cave dark and deep his counsel he keeps -
Fate is this man, yet with a mind which is very deep -
He plans and plots, his foulness to pollute the world
No caves has he little boys or girls
Even the old do not escape his wrath -
His thoughts and doctrine are all against his guilt
He uses God or Allah, call him what you will -
As can excuse, to murder, rape and pill -
Until his struggle is lost or won -
The country where he hides is not the one of his birth -
To them he has brought, misery and hell on earth -
Poor are they but have a right to live -
They need to take, but also need to give
The hand where they live is harsh and unkind -
It is their home, should be a good place to live -
Peace and happiness is what they need -
Not fear, torture, blood and foul deeds -
The horseman of the year apocalypse are riding on their steeds
Encouraging and helping evil to carry out its needs -
To destroy this man, will not be the battle won
He wishes to die, a martyr for all to see
His death will accelerate the final struggle upon this earth -
Good against evil must prevail
Or man will fall beneath the final flare -
The supreme power, call it what you will
Will wait until the world is still -
Its final judgement it will make -
The ring of terror the bringer of all evil
Will finally fall beneath its misty well -
Man is insignificant, a mere tiny pawn -
His time in the universe is nigh
All that it will he is just a sigh

You fools, you would not listen
You would not obey my will -
You are gone, the earth is still
Bold and dark, a desolate place -
Spinning on forever empty into space.

Carl Kemper

Prayer For Children

Have mercy Lord on children the world through,
Pity the little ones who are not told
How you, a child, were born in winter cold
As angels sang; and how you came to die
On a cruel cross below a shadowed sky.
The only hope they have is to know you.

The sun's so golden and the sky so blue,
But there's no lasting peace in earth below.
The world is needing peace, it does not know,
As under that same dazzling sun and sky
Are unloved children who in deserts die;
The only hope of peace they have's in you.

The morning sparkles fresh with rainbowed dew.
Almighty God, who made earth's splendid day,
Dark night for calm and sleep, from love; we pray
That all the children through the world may live
Knowing the wonder love alone can give.
The one great hope of love for all is you.

Diana Momber

STICKS AND STONES

He was a boy who learned to hate
And so it was to become his fate.
In a land that could not start anew,
That place where animosity grew.

In a city that's so walled in
Compressing enmity like a pin.
Pushing through the fabric of time
To the rude coffins placed in line.

And so boxed in by their belief
Negotiation brings no relief.
If eyes are the windows of the soul
Then let them see this terrible toll.

Where mere children throw the stones
And tense soldiers break their bones.
Where suicide is a way of life
And families grow in fear and strife.

H D Hensman

SILENT SPRING

The bittern's boom rings out
less often than the still regular clock
in the church tower. The rock
and roll of gunshot scarers mark the hour,
but bitterns do not shout.

The fen is drained and dry,
and fields are wide. The bittern's boom
no longer carries far enough to reach
a mate. The bitterns gamely try,
but endless silence is

the lonely bittern's fate.
And when, and if, we hear the final boom
of the last bittern,
it will be too late. As with the bittern,
silence is our doom.

Dylan Pugh

WILL YOU STILL TRUST?

You believed when you prayed.
That is what He said to do.
You waited in hope.
Till your loved one died.
Will you still trust?
That He knows what is best
And He always has the final word?
Will you still trust that His love for you is still the same?
Will you still trust that He is kind in everything He does?

Will you still trust?
That He knows your sorrow
He knows your pain?
He will never leave you nor forsake you
Even now in your moment of grief.
He will not let you sink beneath the waves.

Will you still trust when you remember He is a man of sorrow
And acquainted with grief?

Hannah Yaawusuah Adjepong

PIETA

A boy's face
contorted in agony and fear.
His mother lifts him tenderly,
her flowing blue robe
enfolds them both
as she rocks him in anguish.

I turn the television off,
but the image remains
piercing my heart.

Iris Long

LINKING ARMS

We all need one another, of course we always will.
Perhaps more obvious, in the young, old and ill.

Financial reward, capitalist to clown.
So many priorities, are upside down.

Those in the third world, hungry and meek.
One British pound, could keep them for a week.

People are people, working woman or man.
America, Europe or Afghanistan.

There are so many good things, for which we must strive,
No one ever got out, of this world alive.

Like paint working together, across earth's banner unfurled.
If we hope for a future, town, country and world.

E Napper

FOOT AND MOUTH

Cattle burning in a fiery tomb
Lambs - dying in their mother's womb
Frantic squeals of swine - are heard
As they are 'slaughtered' - that's the word!

Farmers - bursting hearts - and crying
Mourning their flocks - dead and dying
Children - can't come home from school
'Stay with Grandma' - that's the rule!

Where are we to go - from here?
What of the future - despair! Fear?
Will cattle and sheep ever graze again?
On pastures - fertilised with pain.

Where is our green and pleasant land?
With death - destruction - gun in hand.

Olga Margaret Moorhouse

GROUND ZERO

Asbestos dust has settled. Flames burn out.
Emergent from the rubble of a dream,
the strangely twisted silvered girders gleam.
Too stunned to think what it may be about,
a man can only ache to hide, and hurt, and shout.
Before him here bleak phoenix icons seem
to rise from the ashes of a mighty scheme -
a city's swagger now displaced by doubt.

In this contorted and imploding world,
the kamikaze are honoured, and reviled;
defiant flags are everywhere unfurled;
there's zero talk of being reconciled.
Another page of history turns - and men
and minds can never be the same again.

Clive Craigmile

DILEMMA!

There are hole and corner conclaves
Concealed in Afghanistan caves
Holding guerilla platoons encaved,
Each attempting to outwit and outbrave
American bombing raids.

Some bombs misaim at wartime targets
Hitting civilian billets.
Reducing homes to minute driblets,
Survivors too frail to run the gauntlet
Wander awry to sunset.

Leaving the dead, dragging the maimed,
Shuffling along, skinny of frame,
Too hungry and weak to be inflamed
Expressionless faces, always the same,
Trundling bundles. Who's to blame?

Who suffers when war is declared?
First disabled and sick ensnared
Taking the brunt of any warfare,
Losing all, joining hordes heading nowhere
In their desperate despair.

Fanatics act before reason,
Followers yoke in unison,
Scission is regarded as treason
Causing death or committal to prison,
Without conscience - Satan's demons!

Dilemma! Anarchists want more
Territory, own religion law
World-wide, their politics, semaphore,
Recognised globally forever more,
We become serfs within our shores.

Hilary Jill Robson

AMERICAN SPIRIT

Stars and stripes within all our psyches,
we that go on for you,
must have courage and will, in the face of fear.
Show terror fails, hatred falls in darkness
to nothing but shadows . . .
Truth stands, rises above
with faith and God's love.
Beyond any shadow - in hope is strength
that will never die.
America's towers fall . . . people so cherished,
so many lives taken,
yet in our hearts and memories,
remain they, our stars now . . .
striped, and forever remembered,
indelible their spirits, and in our minds . . .
though pain and grief in river's ripples
our conscience,
compassion, for each other, an empathy of tears,
washes our souls, in one solidarity now,
to become as one beam of true light
individually, together,
to love of and for each other . . .
America's spirit rises now within
us all . . .

Paul Holland

WHY ISN'T CHRISTMAS CHRISTMAS ANYMORE?

The poor man lies in cardboard city on the street
No pressure worries or deadlines to meet
Cancer victims waiting in beds beside
No future to look to, no secrets to hide
With grim graffiti written on walls
Where do we stand when someone calls?
Why isn't Christmas Christmas anymore?

But something's wrong it's not that clear
We are not filled with good cheer
No children singing in the air
With growing gloom no one cares
The tension is about in all extremes
We are just full of broken dreams
What is there left? Just what's in store?
Why isn't Christmas Christmas anymore?

There is no snow to bring in the cold
With little books and stories to unfold
Goodwill has disappeared and gone away
We don't give our thanks and want to pray
Presents galore are very cheap
And money worries take our sleep
Now meek and mild break the law
Why isn't Christmas Christmas anymore?

There is deep depression on the news
We have all succumbed to winter blues
It's for the kids they want to shout
But do they know what it's all about?
It's sadness all around that we see
As the lights go down on the tree
Happiness has finally found the door
Why isn't Christmas Christmas anymore?

Mike Wetson

LEEK

There is a little town between Morridge and Mow Cop
It used to be a lovely town but now it has gone to pot
If you have not been for years you will just stand and stare
Because there's hardly any historical building's left anywhere.

They knocked down the Golden Lion and the stables at the back
And the old Conservative Club we do miss that
The poor Old George had to come down to widen the road they say
Now the Swan stands out in Mill Street as if to rue the day.

Just a little further down the road many years ago
They built a smashing wall, perfect Whacko
Then a few weeks after without any warning
The whole lot crashed down early one morning.

They built themselves a bus station where the cattle market used to be
And then built a wall and a lot of shops all empty now you can see
The cattle market now is in the middle of Junction Road
So most of the farmers say now 'Straight to Utchiter with this load.'

They have built a swimming baths on Brough Park in a lovely place,
what a lark
If you are well off and have a car you cannot go to the baths in it
Because there is nowhere to park.

May Ward

UNLIKE BEFORE

Turned on the set, broke out in a sweat
I heard it on the News
The world's grown up, 'Forgive' 'Forget'
- the greatest story we've heard yet
We've written off the Third World Debt,
no single nation's under threat
Northern Ireland, Arabs, Jews
I heard
I heard it on the News

It's on the News, it's all about
We've laid it all to rest
No more bloodshed, there's no doubt,
no bombs, no floods, no pain, no drought
Dictators have no filth to spout
It's all around, it's all about
all people on the planet shout
That Peace
Peace is breaking out

No angry fists, no terrorists
The streets are safe to walk
No hate to teach, no poisoned speech
no dreams too far beyond our reach
No politicians from us leach, the leaders practice what they preach
And we're all free
And we're all free to talk

No nuclear threats, no closing nets
A world unlike before
No hate of race in any place
Where words of Love cannot lose face
The persecuted given grace
The trod-on people handed space
Realise the dreams they're born to chase
From oceans shore to shore
The world unlike
With no more war
The world unlike before.

Sparky

POINTLESS ACTS

An insecure world filled with hatred and fear,
Where suffering is rife, and wars never cease.
Where religion and terrorism, fill a world that is clear,
With heartache and sorry, unheard cries for peace.

To solve these problems, that reign in our land,
Famine and hunger, death caused by man.
By educating children, to live in peace, hand in hand,
Creating a world, where people could stand as a clan.

By acting now our world will not die,
Life not death, in a world that knows only peace.
Wiping the tear from the child that cries,
Creating harmony in a world, where wars would cease.

A living memory for two towers so tall,
That in a single, pointless act, where brought to fall.

Andrew Brian Zipfell

SEPTEMBER 11TH 2001 NEW YORK

The twin towers erupt in a flaming ball
Striking terror in the hearts of us all,
Heroic firemen gasping and trying to shout
Five thousand dead, there's no doubt,
Looking for bodies in the twisted, burning embers
That's what a NY fireman remembers,
Police sirens everywhere on the block
People stretchered that cannot walk,
Surely this is not NY City in all its glory
The stunned Americans realise and unfold the story,
Terrorism act that's beyond belief
Even the FBI could not conceive,
The globe shakes with revenge in every man
Destroy Bin Laden and the Taliban,
The Americans unleash awesome fire power
Flattening Kabul, for the twin tower
The Afghan people flee as far as they can
Even through the borders of Pakistan,
No need for funerals or a pyre
Bodies melted with so-called 'friendly fire',
B52 bombers drop their daisies in the caves
Flesh and bone vaporise into early graves,
Back in the western world, financial disasters loom
Companies going bust, when they usually bloom,
Airlines grounded, factories closing down
Even company pensions are making a frown,
How many millions will September 11th have cost?
How many millions of souls will be lost?
The true cost, the world will never be told
Even if Osama Bin Laden lives to be old.

Gus

THE HEROES OF THE DAY

The firefighters, the brave, the heroes of the day.
A sight for sore eyes as the tears are wiped away.
Through rubble and dust and the black of death smoke,
Through the flames of the fires and the people who choke.
They fight through the confusion and the debris on the street,
Working as a team with the people that they meet.
Men and women brave who have a one and only goal,
a mission of survival, saving lives and saving soul.
Burying their fears and thinking only of others need.
Rescuing those feared missing and those who didn't succeed.
As the death toll rises and the survivors are getting low.
The heroes of the day feel as if they're on death row.
Waiting for their punishment and watching others on the road to die,
They keep up the little strength they have
and they keep their hopes up high.
They know it's not looking prosperous
but they believe there's a chance for some
but as they retrieve the dead that they find, their minds and bodies
numb.
Thinking of these innocent people they've found
and who these people are.
They must be family and friends, to us all,
whether from near or from far,
Thinking of those awaiting good news
as they find their precious loved one,
and still these heroes carry on with a gruesome job that must be done.
So a praise must go out to the brave of the day,
for their hearts and strength that they give.
With a blessing for all that they have done,
knowing that they have helped people to live.
Respect to them all over the world for risking their own lives.
Knowing that there are people out there continuing to survive.
All because of the jobs that they do to help them earn a living.
They give their lives and souls to their jobs to keep *our world living*.

Alison Baiton

BOMBED

Twisted metal
by twisted minds,
shattered windows
by shattered blinds.

Bricks, mortar,
concrete, stone,
devastation
to our fabric home.

Buildings, like children
wailing despair,
their dusty tears
filling the air.

Across the world
the images flashed,
of a proud city,
trashed.

Alone, a pillar box survives,
defiant, upright, apart.
Red, bright, standing tall,
a symbol of Mancunian hearts.

Jean

DESTRUCTION OF SOCIETY

I'm afraid in this present society
it is now dark and dismal days
As the milk of human kindness
has begun to drift away.

We have people who are unsociable
who live in nearly every street
Where their victims' complaints are useless
as they suffer from defeat.

Then there is this road rage
where punches can be thrown
There's no longer knights upon the road
as those incidents all are shown.

Old age pensioners are being attacked
for cash they accumulate
Some are left with injuries
which is sad in their frail state.

It is not like in the Thirties
when poverty was rife
As Society was then much friendlier
and was a neighbourly way of life.

Lachlan Taylor

SORROWS AND SMILES

The world is clothed in sorrows and smiles.
I've felt a tear wash down my cheek,
Into others hearts.
I've passed on a smile to a stranger,
On the wayside.
If you get the chance to stop.
Then let us stop, laugh and cry.
This emotion, we can share with millions.
Who can always say.
They've had the time,
To laugh and cry,
This day-long day away.

Charles David Jenkins

DUST SHOWERS

Dust showers fell
Where the margins once stood
And concrete towers
Crouched whilst they could

As, sucked through the nostrils
Of limited joy,
An air of despondency
Found some employ

Strung from the rafters
The visible strain
Of poverty caught
In its mousetrap again

Then the silence of lips
That can ask for no more
An avoidance of stares
As eyes turn to the floor.

Kim Montia

WAR

They call it politics
Whether to kill and whether to maim
What is their aim?

To get rid of the leader so they say
Never mind the civilians who get in the way.

They are the innocent victims of the big row
Which our leaders say is
A just war.

Margaret Jones

WHO'S OUT THERE?

Scorched heat stifles my battered throat and chest.
Mud, plaster, shatters my legs, arms, the rest.
Inhaling, I gasp wincingly for breath.

My ears scream, I hear hysterical laughter.
Babies crying, a boom, a blast, comes near.
Only if I live this story, I'll tell.

Debris flying, stench filling my nostrils.
I shrill a yell, I can't stir, fear prevails.
More blackness fills the air, numbness prevails.

With deep breath,
Help!
Who's out there? I'm struck blind.
Help!
Who's out there? Is there help for mankind?

Lesley J Worrall

YOUR DREAMS

I can hear your dreams playing
through the furrowed brow.
As they wend their way
and sit on pursed lips now.

Your eyes shout their angry words
so loud but I never hear.
All that's left for me to see
is a wet, running tear.

I watch your weary face
casting shadows on my soul.
And sat opposite, I wonder
what's seen in your soup bowl.

Maybe you're remembering
all the times we've had till now.
And perhaps you see it different
but I don't see how.

I think of all those pleasures
that come of two lives as one.
Of how close two people can be
how deep into one become.

I would like to live in ever sunlight
and I can kid myself for days.
But those dreams drowning your face
are not the brightest but the greys.

So as I sit and listen
to woes and piercing doubt.
I'll wait and see the outcome
or is it my turn to shout?

Kim Taylor

SOMEWHERE

In some remote, far distant land
Even as we speak,
Children starve with hunger,
People are tired and weak.
Somewhere in countries never heard
Lives are torn apart,
Times of desperation,
Scenes to touch the heart.
Living with little or no hope,
Plunged to depths of despair,
When we know these things exist
Life really isn't fair.
Things we may take for granted
Food, running water - clear
We have much to be thankful for
We have nothing to fear.

Jennifer Payne

TIME CHANGES NOTHING

Why do I sit and dream
of things I've been shown
but never seen
of times gone by long ago
did I want to be there
no, not I.
Why, because now is my time
no one is perfect
how hard I've tried
sometimes it's hard going
swimming against the tide
in everyone's times it's
been so many
things that went wrong.
Wars and deceit
hunger and sadness
laid at their feet
lives that were taken
lands that belonged
to peoples in far away places
destroyed, left no traces
wiped out complete races.
Why do I sit and dream
because I see what
has gone before
the same is now in store
nothing changes, only faces.

V Anderson

OUR WORLD

God created the world for us to have a life
He could not have known there would be war and strife
Put people on Earth to love one another
Not to hate but be close like sister and brother.
It didn't turn out like that because of selfishness and greed
The human race ignored this and they took no heed
Churches tried to help and join them in their prayers
Politicians also worked with busy world affairs
Will there be an answer - where will it all end?
To family and friends my love I always send.

Ethel Wakeford

WORDS

Words can't describe the pain within
The hurt and destruction, blood that's worn thin
The catastrophe that unfolds before our eyes
All the questions, all the why's.

Words help heal the wounds agape
In our world that's strewn with red tape
The healing's started, although you don't know
As much as you're bleeding and feeling low.

Words are soothing; they reach out and touch
Let the tears flow, however much
Picking on innocence, folk of all ages
Fear, terror, anger, that rages.

Words at this point, become hard to find
Together with love this hatred will bind
United we stand, together we're strong
To fight against evil, and all that is wrong.

Words of anger now prevail
Let them flow freely, empty your pail
Out of your system let it flow
Your inner being will later glow.

Words alongside time, our hearts will heal
The memory of loved ones, cherished, forever in our heart sealed.

Words are precious.

Nigel L Coles

FAITH
(Dedicated to June Gambier)

When times seem really hard
And all it seems is lost
Remember that to win through
Is always worth the cost

So use each day to live your life
And look at things you have
The path ahead has ups and downs
But keep on up the path

For every pathway has an end
And blue skies lie ahead
So keep on going forward
In your steps and in your head

And one day all will be
As when you started out
Far with determination
You can turn your life about

L E Davies

A TROUBLE SHARED

God is all-faithful
Constant and true,
He comforts, soothes
And all sorrows share,
In His strong embrace
Our faith we renew -
And troubles we leave
In His tender care.

Marian Curtis Jones

IN MEMORIUM
(Written on 12th September 2001)

Though they will never walk this earth again,
Or breathe the sun-filled air,
Although they have been taken so rudely from us
Yet we must not give way to despair.

A bright light must always shine before us,
In this dark world of struggling strife.
Always, we must work towards perfect peace
Leading to a better place, a better life.

All nations must join hands together,
Working towards the people's common aim
That we, all together can learn to love,
Although we're different, our thoughts are the same.

So Lord, give us the peace and strength of mind
To live together for the good of all mankind.

Rose-Marie Bonnevier

BETTER TIMES

Everyone hopes for better times
The homeless, the lonely and sad
Something to look forward to
So things don't seem so bad

It will get better in time they say
Progress will create new life
Hollow words to many
It cuts them like a knife

Better times ahead of us
Things will turn about
Just be patient for a while
Please don't scream and shout

But what of those who are hungry
The sick, the old and the dying
It's very hard to say to them
Just hang on, we are trying

Change has to start now
To make up the rhymes
It's no good to give empty promises
Now is for better times

Jeanette Jackson

TROUBLED TIMES

Troubled times are with us now,
You say, 'That's nothing new,'
Regretfully I must agree
Without my wanting to.
If only for a little while
We stood aside to think,
How terrible it is to be
Always on the brink
Of war and its catastrophes,
The suffering that it brings
Thousands find themselves caught up
In many evil things.

Those quick to take the sword in hand
And harm the innocent,
Do battle in the name of God
Such never His intent.
He made a world of plenty
Wealth plundered by the few,
Money with the reins of power,
To right this overdue,
Those eking out a mean existence
Lacking bare resource,
Their children dead from hunger,
A shameful Third World curse.

Just to ease our guilty mind
We give what we can spare,
But mostly it is head in sand
Pretend it isn't there.
And when it is we kneel and pray
That it will somehow go away.

Ellen Thompson

IN TROUBLED TIMES

In troubled times - I rest
In the prayer of rest, that goes like this:
I lay, face down, on the bed - that's best!
Arms folded 'neath face; breath - slow, its kiss

Enters the body God has made,
And I direct my consciousness t' the heart:
Breathing easy, as my body wills, as I lay -
And then I can, make a start,

Thru His Grace to handover care.
And I rest with the breath - in and out . . .
With the out-breath I discharge the snare
Of mine hurt, worried mind, with its doubt.

With the in-breath, sometimes, I call on Him,
And so on, and forth. There must be many ways,
And tho this reads like a hymn:
I bless Him for rest, give Him praise

That, His Spirit shall never let us down:
He guides us thru test and thru trial;
Tho (we) appear stranger than a clown -
With His rest, in the heart, we can smile . . .

Anon

PEACE

In sadness of heart I entered the church
And took my seat in the pew
I knelt awhile in communion with God
Then shouldered my burden anew
Again one day I entered the church
And again I knelt to pray
The peace of God stole into my heart
And abound with me in my way
With hope in my heart I entered the church
And listened again to God's voice
Take courage, and your burden will drop
Hold fast to my hand and rejoice
The church indeed is the House of God
Where all His children may meet
And share together both praise and prayer
And worship at his feet

Joan Patrickson

TROUBLED TIMES

Yes troubled times we live in today,
Oh how we all wish that peace could stay.
In the spring the birds sing their sweet song,
And we all wonder how the world could be so wrong.
Bloodshed and fighting, sadness and tears,
Lonely, frightened people living with fear.
Why such corruption and poverty to human beings,
And such disregard for their thoughts and feelings?
When with a little effort we could all live in peace,
And vandalism and selfishness might all decrease.
A material world without values or morals,
We could surely live together in harmony, not quarrels.

Barbara Ann Barker

A CHILD AT WAR

Hollow eyed, expressionless,
Tight lipped, fires his gun.
I wonder what his thoughts were,
His life, had hardly begun.
Not for him, a ball to kick,
No dog, to take for a walk,
He only knows the killing fields,
And violent war-like talk.
He sleeps in caves, holes or a tent,
Without his mother's kiss,
No tender word of comfort,
What sort of life, is this?
Growing up in fear and hate,
A baby, yet - a man!
Just fodder, for the war machine,
Surviving, as best he can.
Won't someone save these children?
Allow them to live in peace.
Protect them from this evil?
Dear God! Please make war cease.

E M Eagle

EXTREME TERROR

The Americans are shocked and stunned
By the act of terror done
As a nation we have cried
Watching innocent Americans die

They were taken from us
As the horror did unfold
What seemed at first an accident
Was something far more bold

We were powerless to help them
We watched in disbelief
We can only do the decent thing
And share their heartfelt grief

As their allies we must help them
Shoulder to shoulder we must stand
The enormity of this crime
Felt throughout the land

The Americans want their revenge
This we understand
The kind of terror they endured
Was more than underhand

The world's been changed forever
It's not just America that feels the hurt
We've been taught the greatest lesson
We must all be more alert

It's a new kind of terror
Horrific to the core
We choose to help America
Who have no choice but go to war

Lynne Taylor

THE DILEMMA OF LOVE

I searched for your face amongst the crowd,
Could it be you? I called out loud,
Who was it? No, it was not you,
I feel as though my heart had broken in two.

My heart had stood still and missed a beat,
It was suddenly broken in pieces at my feet,
Would it forever be restored?
Into the search my whole being had been poured.

Hope springs eternal, or so they say,
Where are you? Perhaps many miles away.
Are you looking for me, as I look for you?
Many years have passed, I must see it through.

The search will go on till the day I die,
Maybe fate will be kind and tell me why?
Perhaps, oh perhaps, you'll be waiting for me,
Only then, and only then, will I be free.

Irene Greenall

MY MAN'S GONE TO JAIL

You're in jail, I am not,
I live free, but I haven't forgot,
Even though you are locked,
You're still the only one I've got,
Even though I'm here and you're not,
I can still feel you in my heart making me hot,
I just want you to know I haven't lost the plot.

And even though we are far apart,
You are still near me within my heart,
I still feel for you now like I did at the start,
And when it comes to men, you will always get top marks.

I don't think you will ever know,
How much I miss you so,
Every day without you I'm sad and low,
Junior why did you have to go?

Shantel Faure

A PLEA TO SLEEP

Oh, Morpheus come and blind these eyes
Close these red and weeping windows.
Rest this weary spirit
This tired head with only worry in it.
This tensioned spine, these aching limbs
The lungs that fight to feed the heart
That between them lies.
How the body sighs.

Oh, Morpheus come and droop these lids
Cover the soft, brown irises
That seek but cannot find
The images of lost love.
Cover this wrecked frame
With your special balm
To blossom forth a new flower.
Oh Morpheus come and blind these eyes
For just a precious hour.

J Aldred

GREENHOUSE

There is a greenhouse overheating,
Plants and animals are shrinking,
The festival of trees
Is now awake for each dead zone.

Ice caps are melting, Arctic disaster
A snow-covered world slides into the sea
Iceberg hits titanic Earth
Atlantis revisited.

So much damage has been done
Earth scientists knew the score,
They speak, but who hears?
A shift of attitude is needed.
This threat is very real.

We are all to blame
Our ravages cut so deep,
Earth is crying from every wound
Mankind has inflicted.
Can we rise to this challenge?

Our children's future
Demands that we do.

Ian Barton

FARMER BROWN'S SWANSONG

No longer the scythe in sunlight glistens
As it did in days long ago.
The horse no longer pulls the plough
Its gait is much too slow.
Man would work from dawn till dusk
While tilling over the soil,
Moving on from farm to farm
His life an endless toil.

In this modern era,
On Lincolnshire's farming land
Tractors and combine harvesters
Work together in a band,
Collecting in the wheat
Or planting out the seed
The work moves ever forward
At an accelerated speed.

Machines earn farmers a fortune,
That's what people thought,
They do not realise that -
There's a battle being fought.
Farmer Brown must sell his land -
His sheep his cattle his grain.
The lots go under the hammer
As a bullet enters his brain.

J A Silkstone

THE ASHEN SHROUD

On wings of terror death hung like a cloud
when evil struck its blow so inhumane
that thousands fell wrapped in ashen shroud
and shocked the world in suffering and pain.
Can hatred be so ruthless and so vile
to plot to kill in such barbaric style?

Eleventh of September, zero one -
a date to be remembered for all time.
We've turned the page . . . a new life has begun -
the world against the transgressors of crime!
We cannot spend our lives in constant fear
of losing all we love and hold most dear.

We are at war! A war we're fighting blind
against a dedication so extreme!
Our children need a future! We must find
the masterminds of this callous regime.
The fog is thick but we will find a way
to pave with peace, the future world's highway.

Joy Saunders

THE WORLD TRADE CENTRE
(Eleventh Of September 2001)

Once again in the name of religion the world mourns
And innocent people sadly become pawns
Pawns in a game that only death can win
But would God sanction this terrible sin
With no word of warning danger threatens
As the skyline in New York changed in seconds

The 11th of September such a sad day
It was absolute carnage to die that way
First one plane hit a tower, it exploded with a bang
They were not sure at this time if it was a terrorist gang
It was soon apparent when the second was blown
The world watched with horror as the pictures were shown

Another target was the pentagon that was a plane too
Then one crashed in Pittsburgh and the death toll just grew
The towers collapsed and hope faded away
It was clear there would be more dead than alive this day,
There were air crews, passengers and workers alike
Firemen and visitors lost under the strike

Relatives wait and pray, one wonders how they cope
Some got calls from loved ones, saying there's no hope
I hope the one who did this deed is brought to mind
There's no place in Heaven or Earth for his kind
This atrocity shook the world, it could mean World War Three
He must be caught he must be stopped if mankind is to be free

Celia Law

WHAT IS WAR?

I looked into a child's eyes.
I was horrified.
This is what I saw -
Aeroplanes dropping big bombs,
Ships with big guns shooting fire,
Homes falling to the ground,
People running all over the place.
Shouting and screaming, crying,
Dropping to the ground,
Some not getting up,
Just lying there in pools of blood
Running and running.
The rest of the people running into fields,
Running and screaming
Along dirt tracks.
I looked into the child's eyes
And saw -
Misery
Torture and death -
No laughter, no smiles
Just hunger and starvation.
This is what I saw
In the child's eyes.

Maureen Powell

CEASEFIRE

Such a fragile peace
That British troops were sent
Out to Macedonia,
Weapons to collect.

Such a fragile peace,
Their land rovers were stoned.
First night there, one sapper died.
Will all the rest come home?

Such a fragile peace,
In this latest Balkan war,
Let's pray that it will hold
Like others gone before.

Joyce Walker

OUR HONEYMOON

Our marriage was a large affair,
Many people came, I was so excited,
On our very special day;
Our honeymoon was in North Wales;
The hotel was very large.
There was a special place we went,
Where there was a little stream.
The stones were easy to walk along,
The bridge was very low;
We loved the little stream so much,
And not a soul we'd see.
The water was so clean and clear,
We would sit upon the stones
And paddle right across the stream.
The water comes a long way down the mountain,
And water becomes quite strong,
It would hit the stones and make a noise.
We would sit upon the stones,
And paddle across the stream.
The water trickles a long way down,
From mountains all around.
What a lovely stream He made.

Heather Ann Breadnam

THE STATE OF THE WORLD

I'm asked yet again,
'What do you think of the state of the world?'

I close my eyes
And images of the fallen towers
Enter my head
People crying for lost family and friends
People crying for all those innocent lives lost
People crying

I close my eyes
And images of children scared to go to school
Enter my head
Army with guns protecting them
Protecting them from stones
Protecting them from their neighbours
Protecting them

I close my eyes
And images of starving people
Enter my head
Trying to make a life for themselves
Trying to make the most of what they have
Trying to live

I open my eyes and reply
'The world is a very scary place to be at the moment.'

Lindsey Brown

Our World

How privileged are we to see, the leaves and blossom on the trees,
To see the clouds in the sky above, or hear the cooing of the dove.
The grass so green and sea so blue, are everyday things to me and you.
Yet in the future what will they see, will these be a lake let alone a sea,
Will they have grass or just white sand? Will there even be music
                                                            or brass band?
A glass dome covering our world, for the ozone layer has
                                                    burned and gone.
We didn't treat our planet right, or stop the destruction before too long.
The rubbish tips, the landfill site. Could have recycled more in the past.
How many things did we throw or dump that could have
                                                    helped others out?
If we turned over a new leaf now and helped to stop the
                                                    tumbling mound.
Would we change things for the future kids so they can kick
                                                    a ball in the streets.
They can breathe the nice fresh air and swim in the lakes and sea:
                                                    the water pure.
To sit upon a sandy beach without cutting skin on glass and
                                                    ripped Coke tins.
So when we go out to have some fun, we should take our litter
                                                    home: take more care.

A M Williamson

CIVILISATION

When man looked at this world
And the goodness therein,
He wondered at first, why there should be sin,
He looked at the sky, he looked at the trees,
He looked at the land, he admired the seas.
He looked beyond the clouds and sighed
'Whoever You are, whatever You are
Thank You Lord.'
Then he discovered that this world is round
He had a bright urge for new lands to be found
He started to stray to faraway places
Sadly he started to wear two faces.
He developed the taste for milk and honey,
The time had come for mankind to have money
And then came the need for more and more.
Now look at the difference between rich and poor,
Now look at the world's needs
Caused by our greed,
Now look at the wars and look at the scars,
In order for one man to have ten shares
Nine must go without whilst always in tears.
May God give us grace to be led by wisdom
For us to get a fair share of the Kingdom.

Dalsie Mullings Powell

IN TROUBLED TIMES

A child's eyes full of fear,
dying of hunger,
people killed or tortured
for the wrong colour
of their skin,
for the wrong odour
of their beliefs.

Our earth depleted,
animals slaughtered.
Greed and envy spreading like cancer.
Each death, each loss
is a part of me
I grieve for, lost for ever.
'Save our planet,' I hear children plead.

Today's papers scream
'Retaliation!'
Children still go to their school
of violence.
Toxic consumerism
poisons our lives;
and war crimes go unnoticed.

Pandora's box,
you seem more and more fragile.
When the lid springs up
all the world's troubles
come tumbling out,
and children are crushed.
Terror explodes, breeding hate.

Can hope still lie hidden
inside Pandora's box?

Antoinette Marshall

LET THERE BE PEACE UPON EARTH

Let there be peace upon this Earth,
The unity that protects our worth,
What about the millions of people,
Who are needing love and humanity,
Where land means the thought of,
Of togetherness not the talk of wars,
Though just getting along together,
For the thought of just getting along,
With one another,
Also means that we can show we can,
Mix in other societies,
Lord please help us see that falling out,
With the largest powers is as lethal,
As the aftermath of the treacherous war zones,
We do not have a look at or think,
Of everything we need,
So I pledge this need for worldwide prayer,
To be noticed all over this globe of ours,
For many of us can see and live in peace.

C Hush

LIVING WITH MEMORIES

Ten years now past
As I write these words
To be mirrored in my mind
Bringing back to me
The years that used to be
Life's pleasures now left behind
Her photographs around my room
Brings me brightness every day
I often watch our family films
Since death took my wife away
Sometimes a sadness does appear
To remind me of my brief
Why? The question floods my mind
Making her passing beyond belief
But there is a life still to live
In helping others meet their pain
Discussing joys each shared in life
And those memories that remain
Moments treasured, laughter, fun
Cloud the memories to one's mind
My joy to life, memories of my dear wife
Life's gift of her treasured time.

E L Hannam

THINK OF THE CHILDREN
(This poem was read out on Berkshire Radio
on National Poetry day)

I pray to Lord Jesus in Heaven
As I kneel by the side of my bed,
For all the little children I pray
Before too much blood is shed.

I am only a little child Lord
Only seven years old,
I pray for all the children like me
Who might never live to be old.

I love my Mum and Dad, Lord
And I know they love me too,
Please don't let there be a war
Let people be peace-loving like you.

I know there are a lot of bad people
And they should be punished for their sin,
But not the whole wide world, Lord,
That won't make anybody win.

I'm sorry I've started crying,
I'm usually quite tough.
I'll sure miss all my mates and my football and stuff.
I've got a great bedroom and I'll miss all the fun,
Especially my computer and my Man United shirt I won.

I pray to you Lord Jesus in Heaven,
I pray for all little children like me,
Because we haven't lived our lives yet
All we want is love, peace and harmony.

Just like you teach us Lord Jesus
If I grow up I want to be like you.
Happy and peaceful and gentle
We'll teach the world a thing or two.

Please watch over my family
And of course our old dog, Ben,
Who send you all their love
And I say thank you Lord for them.

Amen.

Peter (aged 7)

Anthony Hall

HOLOCAUST 2001

The Untermenschen
Cower in their crowded ghetto room
Whilst armed thugs
Of the current Master Race
Strut the street outside,
Howling insults and threats.

Master Race snipers,
For their sport
Pick off 'Untermenschen' workers,
As they go about their tasks
In their olive groves.

Why does a race
That has suffered so much agony
As the target
Of enduring race hatred
Behave in this way?

Surely, by their actions
They validate in their own eyes,
If not in mine,
Their own persecution
And so betray their martyrs
Of sixty years ago?

Perhaps it's like child abuse,
Today's abuser
Was yesterday's abused.

Brian Edwards

I'M COMING BACK

I feel so afraid - my life is a mess
Up to my eyes in doubt and distress
My life seem so worthless so utterly bleak
Can I keep going I'm so terribly weak.

I look back in shame at the things I have done
The sins I've committed - I've nowhere to run
What must God think as he looks down on me
As he witnesses Satan laughing with glee?

I remember the days when I knew how to pray
If only I knew how to do so today
And yet as I tremble thoughts enter my mind
Are they from Jesus - Is he really that kind?

I remember the Bible, the stories therein
The prodigal son - the forgiveness of sin
I look up to Jesus, is it too late for me?
I've fallen so far I can only just see.

'It's never too late' comes the cry from above
My father and I are abounding with love
If Satan is winning and you're on the rack
Remember my promise - I'm coming back.

Tony Taylor

CLINICAL DEPRESSION
(A man who has been there and back again many times!)

All those yesterdays conspire to bring your stresses to the boil
Your self-belief so very low shrinks in panic to recoil.
A night of fractured nightmare sleep, drenched in shivering sweat,
It comes again, that demon fear, you'd long prayed to forget.

Then comes the dawn . . .

Your ice-chilled brain now views all through a veiled dark-clouded eye,
Despite all efforts to contain this Hell, still you want to die.
Stare for ageless hours, nothing moving, no thoughts nor focused sight,
Whilst quivering cold yet streaming sweat, you've lost all will to fight.

The dreaded blackness bedrapes your soul, that living-zombie shroud,
Dry-cough retching cramps your body, whilst your mind still disavows
. . . Blame for this bleak stark lonely state to which you now have come,
The inner 'you' longs to nurse at the breast of your long-dead mom!

'Enough' you cry to no one, 'where's an end to this raw terror?'
Those around tut disapproval, '. . . just pull yourself together!'
But how . . .? But when . . . ? Right now . . . ? What then?
Hopes long gone with dreams of peace.
All you seek from this mind tunnel . . . is a moment's sweet release . . .
From this 'black dread!'

Kim Swales

THAT FATAL DAY

He stood leaning on the old farm gate his dog Bracken by his side,
And gazed at empty sheds and yard, with unbelieving eyes.
No living animal in sight, roaming the fields around,
Just an awful deathly silence, nothing to make a sound.

His mind went back those forty years when his father passed away.
He'd decided then to start a herd of milking cows somehow,
And so from small beginnings, through years his herd had grown,
At dairy shows he'd always won, and so become well-known.

He gazed once more across the yard where he'd milked his
cows each day.
Then turned and with his faithful dog, he slowly walked away,
For so quickly had things happened, which he'd never understand,
And tears ran down the weathered cheeks of this sad and broken man.

Dinah Court

FOREVER

For ever is a day that is eternally long,
We cram our love, our hatred often being wrong,
In a mere day that seems eternally long.

Time nor tide will wait for no one,
Nor do we have time to rectify our wrong,
Done to others without hindsight. A dismal song.

No matter what you believe,
Capitalism will be our downfall in the long run,
So my peers let loose, have some fun.

For tomorrow is a disaster which we cannot overcome.
Make hay while the sun shines, try to belong.
For ever is only a day that is eternally long.

Jay Baker

GLOBAL WARMING

The greenhouse effect in media
Is what we see and hear.
I don't know what can be done
But it fills me full of fear.
Not for myself, nor for the old,
For we have had our time.
But for the young, the not yet born,
I pen this mournful rhyme.
The rising sea from melting ice
Will overrun the land.
Where will they live, the not yet born,
With nowhere left to stand.
The population, rising still,
Will find much less to eat,
When farming land is then a sea,
The rest destroyed by heat.
The blazing forests in Brazil
Have made the world so poor.
Car exhausts and CF gas
And farmers burning straw.
The burning rays from the sun
Will mean they never freeze,
But better shiver in the cold
Than shiver with disease.
The water, full of nitrates,
No longer fit to drink.
The children of the future,
I wonder what they'll think.
Make the most of what we have,
This world of ours will die.
For the unborn of the future
I can only cry.

Harry Gill

THE MINERS' STRIKE

He pulls off his boots, his helmet and his jacket,
The kids are going mad . . . making such a racket,
Watching for a moment, his heart is filled with pride,
As the eldest teaches junior, his bike to properly ride,
It wasn't bought brand new, as money had been tight,
Through standing on the picket line (we put up such a fight!)
Strength we had in numbers, and support from many more,
Charity and handouts, to keep the rent man from the door,
Days turned into weeks, and the months grew steadily worse,
Not a fat chance of surviving, without money in the purse,
The government wouldn't listen, they didn't give a damn!
Well go to Hell the lot of you! Go to Hell and scram!
We brought you to your knees, slowly turning out the lights,
No fires or fuel to keep you warm, in the darkened winter nights
Through cold and damp we stood our ground, illusions all in tatters,
Well go to Hell the lot of you! You're all as mad as hatters!

Now we've risen from the ashes, and the coal is burning bright,
The lantern from his helmet, his ever-guiding light,
So as he pulls on his boots, his helmet and his jacket,
Tying up his laces, taking rest upon the cracket,
His thoughts are of the future, for the children of tomorrow,
Did we ever really win, did it rid us of our sorrow?
Disillusionment and despondency, and with all the tea in China!
In my heart I know, no child of mine, will ever be a *miner!*

Jan Hall

THE VISION

I heard the sounds of wartime: cries of terror and fear.
I saw the blue skies darken and the dust engulf the air.
I touched the shattered bodies and inhaled the stench of death.
And, as this scene unfolded, I watched with bated breath!

I heard the sound of sirens and saw the lights of blue.
I watched the sick and wounded unloaded in a queue.
I saw the glazed doors sliding, and read the written sign -
'We apologise for closing. There isn't room inside.'

I heard the wails of panic rise from the stricken crowd.
Awareness dwelled amid them: no treatment would be found.
I sensed their desperation, their suffering and their pain,
And listened as they shouted, 'It's the government to blame!'

I thought about this vision and questions filled my mind.
What if this really happened? What treatment would we find?
How would the sick be cared for in a country of neglect?
This land of hope and glory;
Where hope is all that's left!

Sandra Wolfe

SORROW

Today, once more, I felt your pain,
dark, sad eyes, still empty and lost,
still trying to reap the cost,
of sorrow.

I too, was a part of that I know,
a small, but perhaps a caring part,
but God, it was over long ago,
when we touched, and used the heart,
of sorrow.

Fly free, while life is worth living,
your soul must start to beat again,
the grief you gave was worth the giving,
you are here, still to beat the pain,
of sorrow.

J S Liberkowski

PONDER AND WISH

To sit and watch the world destroyed
Is everybody's fate.
No one cares enough
To change.
It's too much like hard work.

To care for animals and trees and flowers
Is old-fashioned and sissy,
To some, maybe,
To most, perhaps.
But then of course
There's me.

Am I alone? It seems that way.
But surely not completely.
There must be others somewhere here.
Or maybe I'm not of this planet!

That must be it!
Or maybe I've been born too early.
The far future has to be better,
Should I bide my time and wait
Until next time round?

After death comes more life,
Than we can never know,
We *must* learn by our mistakes,
To come back for the better.

So take time out to think and see,
What we humans are doing.
We must unite and join against
The animal executioners.

Be it meat, fur, vivisection or 'sport'
It must be stamped out *for ever!*

Maxene Huntley

A World In Conflict

Why must we hate, why must it be?
Look back through history and you will see
A legacy of war and dying
People hating and people crying
Look at Ireland and what could be
North and south together in unity
Look at Africa white and black
If only we could turn the clock back
And Bosnia I don't understand
As this was once a lovely land.
Until the politicians had their say
And war and fighting came to stay,
Afghanistan, what more can be said
With children dying and thousands dead.
Every nation is born equal, woman and man
We should try to help each other while we can
Forget our politics, religion and creed,
And let's learn to give in this time of need
And make our world a better place to be
All nations as one living in harmony

Robert Beach

CASUALTY

The other day images of war long gone
Spilled from the television invading
My living room with stark monochrome mud,
Torn earth, barbed wire, soldiers and blood.

And distant memories awoke within,
Not of war as such but of Auntie Nell
My father's aunt lying in a neat white bed,
Slipping from life without regret or dread.

We had laughed and played, she had made me dolls'
clothes and sometimes necklaces of bright beads.
Me, all unknowing of war's brutal cost,
And the son she had once had and lost . . .

Minutes before the eleventh hour on
The eleventh day of the eleventh month . . .

Margaret Hibbert

NEVER SUCH INNOCENCE

I lie in the sun amongst the grass
Where others strive to build their wrath,
To fight and take victory there,
Never to be concerned, never to care.
I lie, heart still beating, watching those boys
Fighting for country (running with guns) as if they were toys
On a plastic map spread across the floor,
Playing together and forgetting the war,
Just like toy soldiers row upon row,
Not knowing their fate or the way to go.
And at last as I die, my heart speaks aloud:
Never such innocence - fighting proud.

Jessi Ray

THE CALL

Don't you be discouraged
If you lose your way.
Jesus said, 'I'm with you -
Come what may.
In these troubled times,
Through the darkest night
Put your trust in me,
I will be your light.
I will be your shelter,
Though the mountains fall.
Just believe in me -
And I will hear your call.'

Ken Price

A CONTRIBUTION TO WORLD PEACE
(For Maureen)

She arrived the day and hour she'd said she would,
Straight from New York. Advised to cancel, she had said,
'My flight is booked; I'll go.'
But she had been in the street
When she saw the aircraft coming in and thought,
'My goodness, that's low!
That's going to crash!'
Turned the corner,
'Into my building,' heard the smash.
Took it for an accident, but then there was another,
'That's odd.'
Turned the television on and learned The Pentagon
Had been hit. Then she understood.
'My God.'
Still a little throaty from the dust,
She asked, ' Must history repeat?'
What should, what could
One do?' I said, 'Just
Take care to deal in equity and kindliness with whom we meet
Keep one corner sweet.' A few days after
She had left, I noticed Alexander,
My big ginger cat with white throat and feet,
Seated erect, my hens, brown Lucy
And the pearly bantam, Millicent
Nestled behind him without fear.
They made a picture and I took a snap
And sent a print to her, entitled on the back,
'An oasis of peace in a naughty world.'
It worked a treat.

Jean Overton Fuller

IN TROUBLED TIMES

The world is in turmoil, men fighting men with sophisticated
killing machines
Causing suffering and sorrow, confusion and horror, spilling
hatred unseen.
Where has the love gone, the gentle forgiveness Jesus imparted
long ago?
Have we forgotten the quiet compassion on people and creatures
he would bestow
Why do we humans evoke such pleasure from hurting and maiming our
fellow men
Why can't we accept that life is a treasure - a gift so precious we may
not see again?
Now Christmas is near us with its many blessings, children sing carols
around the tree.
Bells ring out their happy message around the world - over land
and sea.
Proclaiming God's love for all his people he is stretching our his hand.
'Peace on Earth!' Oh! Please let it happen
for every child in every land.

Elsie Francis

MAN'S INJURY TO HIMSELF

His tears are still wet upon his face
His mother in sorrow bends with no grace
In agony looks around
Where can real peace be found?

Where once there were towers tall and proud
Then terror came right through the cloud
Lives were busy of commerce inside
And a 1000 hearts were broken and died.

Where once the streams were pure and clean
So beautiful they were, are now not seen
And animals once known are now extinct
While others too are on the brink.

Religion has had its glory in time
The hurt and pain has been yours and mine
With bloodshed has ruled with a rod
Now judgement upon her will come from God.

Then the time of war will be no more
The Earth will be blessed you can be sure.
As Peace will rule this Earth sublime
As God's Kingdom rules for all time.

Victoria Sisam

SAVAGE WINGS

Demonising the skies of Manhattan
came a howling wind of assassination
twin bastions of the big democracy
were cruelly smashed into infinity

Who will pick up the pieces now
when the power lines are down
a fresh morning was blown away
tonight dirty water rains

A new hill sprawls at the end of the street
the Big Apple peels
bleak visions for a civilised eye
structures of freedom crumble and die

So many fathers, so many sons
mothers and daughters so many won't be coming home
their working day started and ended forever
on the blackest of days the eleventh of September.

Gerard Wilson

MESSAGE FROM THE ECO WARRIOR

The lone Eco Warrior
    stands at the edge of doom
his fair long hair
    blowing in the wind.

A rainbow-coloured cape
    flowing from his shoulders.
A beautiful crystal glowing
    and sparkling at his throat.

Gently his friends plucked
    the strings of his guitar.
Then his heart's lament
    spiralled in the air.

Will you hear me people
    of this planet Earth?
Will you hear my song?

Will you stop the violence?
    Will you stop the strife?

Will you stop the plunder?
    Will you stop the greed?

Listen! Mother Earth is weeping
    Her children have gone astray.

Animals are dying out
    plants and trees are withering
under clouds of poisonous fumes.

The ozone layer - there
    to protect us from the sun
is thinning, leaving us to burn.

The delicate Eco system
    so cleverly planned
is crumbling, is vanishing
    before my disbelieving eyes.

The Eco Warrior lifts
    his head to the sky
eyes streaming with tears
    and begs the angels to help.

Please let light flow
    into people's souls.
Open their hearts
    before it is too late.

Let enlightenment and understanding
    take the place of scepticism.
Let love and compassion take
    the place of hate and scorn.

Tell them they were guardians
    of this, their planet Earth.
This beautiful garden
    created to give them joy.

The angels came and
    brought their message.
A few heard and were filled with light.

But many scorned the message
    and continued to plunder.

Animals are still crying in pain
    trees are felled and forests stripped bare.

Oh foolish people, can you not see?
    When there are no more animals or trees
When Mother Earth is slowly dying,
    can you not see that you will be no more?

The Eco Warrior lifts his arms in supplication
  once more his pleading song streams forth.

Will you hear me people of this planet
  will you hear me before it is too late?

Or carry on in the same old way
  and see your future die . . .?

Brigitta D'Arcy

DON'T FORGET ME

I run my hand
through the dust of this damned land
breaking the crust.
What seems like mud
is the blood of my brother
as another
falls foul to Bin Laden.
Icy winds turning and burning me to the core
I can't take anymore
I don't understand
how this hell
reminds me of Brighton sand
No rain for what seems a thousand years
Why am I here
In no-man's land?
An endless rocky plain
driving me insane
with its continuous monotonous depths
rock after rock after rock.
Let me take stock
of my life
trying not to think of my wife, and son
Memories bring pain
Don't feel the same
Another day is done.
Don't forget me
Don't let me pass out of your heart
remember I'm part
of your destiny.
As you walk on Brighton's beach
I will reach out and touch you again.

L Johnson

WHOSE FAULT IS IT THEN? (A RENGA)

Earth is our planet,
In Milky Way's galaxy,
But we're killing it.

Our use of CFC sprays
And burning of fossil fuels

Creates too much CO^2
And holes our ozone layer

Which protects us from the sun.
We chop down our rainforests

Which rejuvenate the Earth,
And then say it's not our fault!

But have we learned our lesson?
No - we continue to smoke

And poison our atmosphere,
Speeding up our planet's doom.

We suppose ourselves to be
Creatures of intelligence

But still we hasten our demise
By killing our salvation.

Mick Nash

A DAY ON THE FARM

There's a family gathering down on the farm
Could it be a birthday or wedding?
No, it's not tears of joy they are shedding
It's the day they've been dreading
And now it's finally here.

The bewildered farmer
Sees his home overrun
By white coats with guns
The digging has begun
And he just feels so helpless.

The lonely farmer walks out into his yard
The strangers have gone
The trucks have moved on
'What have I done wrong?'
He cries as he looks around.

The desolate farmer wanders into his field,
And into his shed.
Where his stock slept and fed
And now lay shot dead
He breaks down with his head in his hands.

He stays there 'til dark seeing hope on the horizon
But there's only the glowing hot fires
Of stinking funeral pyres
Sending up clouds of death and despair.

His wife comes to find him
Not knowing what to say
She's been crying all day
Now she leads him away
From the scene that is breaking their hearts.

Karen Cook

NEW WAR, OLD WAR

It's a new kind of war they tell me
From the box in the corner, TV.
It may be short, it could be long
We have to fight it, to right the wrong
Of terrorism.

There won't be a marked-out battlefield
The enemy will be hard to find
For he won't be wearing a uniform
To identify his kind
Of terrorism.

This is a new kind of war they tell me
From that box in the corner, TV.
But the same old bombs are descending
Though a new race of children cry
And bodies still sprawl a'bleeding
Under the same old sky
In a war that seems never-ending
For the soul of humanity.

So Jehovah or Jesus or Allah
Whatever your name might be
Krishna or Buddha, wherever you are
Look down with pity and heal the scars
Left by the age-old endless wars
Waged by humanity.

Meg Gilholm

THE TWO MONOLITHS

They cast a shadow from the sky like eagles on their prey.
Two monoliths stretching forth, living giants,
shining glass reflecting in the eagle's eyes.
Then the eagle struck at the monolithic giant.
Cries of shame raged forth, then crashing down, the giant
                                        stood no more.

Echoes of war rang out from coast to coast, death lay at its helm.
The beating of war sallied forth,
phoenix like the eagles rose from where the giants lay.
One by one they roared and flew over land and sea.
In their eyes revenge lay deep.
The land they sought was barren with war.
Each eagle swooped regardless of its prey,
for the foe lay with the innocent upon that barren day.

Philip Nugent

PLAYING GOD?

Mary Shelley's 'Frankenstein'
was prophetic. Cloning:
sheep, pigs,
humans;
where will it all end? I,
like others, dread
to think. Should we even meddle
at all? I do not
claim to know. We
look to philosophy of science, and
philosophy of religion
for the answers,
and we get
a lot
more
questions. A lot more
headaches, and admissions
to A and E, and
psychiatric wards. Still,
we have to try
to understand, don't we?
Don't we?

Paula Puddephatt

BEFORE TOO LONG

In a downward spiral we are going,
Children of tender years, involved with crime.
Always someone to whom we are owing,
But how can we escape this moral grime?

Worries seem to build with each passing day,
More bills, more wants and with no end in sight.
Youngsters not happy being told to play,
Whole world seems to share this terrible plight.

Nobody seems settled with what they've got,
National debt always is on the increase.
Especially youths expect all the lot,
And through these troubled times, wars do not cease.

Hope there's a way to escape this awful fate,
Again acquire good standard of living.
Solution must be found before too late,
Become once more nation of forgiving.

S Mullinger

WHAT CHANCE A CHILD!

A child of today, what are its chances;
In a world of very fragile circumstances?
Feuds, conflicts, wars that won't abate;
What chances a child? In a world full of hate!

Dictators come, and tyrants may go,
But who's left behind, in the afterglow?
The child, trying desperately to understand,
Why all the grown ups are destroying the land!

Bombs exploding, fighting all around,
Forcing the child, to hide underground!
To survive on scraps, whatever it can find,
What chance a child, with all this on its mind?

Perhaps one day, all wars will cease!
And all the world, will join in peace!
Perhaps the child, will, one day, know joy!
And live its life happy, a contented girl or boy!

R Ninnis

TROUBLES

When troubles hit you, hit you hard
Or sorrows come your way,
You'll have excuses for angry words
Or weeping every day.

Excuse indeed but better still
To keep on keeping on,
Your smiling face will scarce a trace
For when your love has gone.

D Sheasby

JEREMIAH 33 V 3

('Call to me and I will answer you and show you great and mighty things which you do not know')

I have done so much for you
Of which you do not know
Protected you in troubled times
And held you in my arms

The times you thought that no one cared
And no one heard your cries
I was always there beside you
But you never heard my sighs

My child you are, my child you know
Let me your Father be
Will you come into my presence
And sit awhile with me

I will tell you of my love for you
That you are precious in my sight
Pour out my blessings upon you
And give you abundant life.

Ann Langley

WILL IT EVER END?

Dear God,
It's been a long time
Since I could look you in the eye.
It's hard
To put your faith
In the will of Heaven
When you're too sad
To think what to say;
And every day
The world's bad news is endless.
And mine is so small
In the grand scheme of things.
But we're trying
To come back,
And only ask you
To keep us safe,
Until the day
When we can all be together
In happiness and light.

Andy Bryan

PALESTINE WOMAN

Her arms were long and scrawny, the skin was paper dry ,
With hands outstretched she pleaded to those who passed her by.
Sunk deep in their sockets, her black eyes scarce alive,
Just another brown-skinned woman, begging to survive.

She cared naught for racial conflict, it was all she'd ever known,
And like other countless women, she too was now alone.
Like them she screamed in torment as she brought forth each son,
Knowing well she'd scream again, as she lost them one by one.

But in a patriarchal state, where women have no say,
Men blame it on the other side, the enemy must pay.
They care nothing for the helpless, the innocent or frail,
To throw a rock, or fire a gun, will prove that he is male.

Why won't they get the message, when will they ever heed
The reasoning of women, by giving them the lead.
So that future mothers will never have to cry,
'Alms for the love of Allah, Alms until I die.'

Joyce Greaves

LET JUSTICE BE DONE

This was our island home - 'Land of the Free'
A place of peace and safety for people like you and me
But over recent decades we've seen this image change,
To graffiti, rape and pillage, and see our morals all deranged.

Our legal system which once was the envy of the world
Has been laughed at and degraded at which dirt and lies
have been hurled
But when are we going to stop the rot and bring the criminals to justice?
It must be *now!* Or never hold our heads up high
dispensing legal justice.

We've seen the arsonist do his work
We've seen our cathedrals burnt
And yet the villains walk away without a single hurt
But when, oh when, will we all stand up and shout it is 'enough'
And let English justice stand, and show it can be true and *just?*

The *do-gooders'* have had their day
And the minorities have had their say
But the old saying of 'Spare the rod and spoil the child'
Has been proven right - *our justice today is far too mild.*

Douglas Peet

SAD MEMORIES

It used to be a lovely walk along Pickwood Lane,
Now everything has gone, it will never be the same.
The trees where the children played their games
Gone forever -only sad memories remain.

There are a hundred houses built there now,
Where the green fields used to be.
Gone are the sheep and the cows,
The rabbits and squirrels we do not see.

Nothing is the same - who's to blame?
The so and so's who call it progress.
Between you and me there is a name,
'The Concrete Jungle' - what a mess.

May Ward

MISSILES OF DESTRUCTION

When I close my eyes,
shadows march across
the windows of my mind,
bringing grief
so deep, so painful,
I cannot sleep.

I see the black image of a
streaking plane on a backdrop
of blue sky, aimed
like a poisoned arrow
at the heart of
an unsuspecting people.

Numb, uncomprehending
Another armed missile flies past
Bringing more devastation,
More anguish, more Death,
By fire, explosion and, in the end,
The collapse of innocence.

Thousands die in an instant,
For a belief that has been altered -
By a few soul-less traitors -
From teachings of peace and love,
To hatred of the world - their
Ignorance profound.

Forgiveness cannot be chosen - yet.
The pain is still unbearable.
Retribution must be had
To avenge so many,
Lost amongst the fiery rubble
Of a Religion gone mad.

Polly Davies

11TH SEPTEMBER

Those Al-Qua'ida fanatical monsters
Who hijacked the passenger planes
How could they be so evil
To crash into the Twin Towers that day

All the passengers on that flight
They were so very brave
And out of all the thousands in the towers
A minority of them were saved

The nations have joined together
Our leaders will have their say
They will fight this war against terror
Osama Bin Laden and his Taliban will pay

We don't wish to cause any suffering
To the Afghani civilians there
Because unlike Osama Bin Laden
The United Nations care

But there's nothing else we can do
There is no other way
We've got to stop Bin Laden
And make the Taliban pay

Osama Bin Laden thinks he's safe
In his mountain lair
But the elite troops of the SAS
Will seek and find him there

We must preserve our way of life
So justice we will find
Rid the world of terror
Like Osama Bin Laden and his kind.

Elizabeth Mayes

MAN'S PRAYER

Love's all around, it's plain to see
But also hatred, oh how can this be?
Some will succeed and some will fail
Why don't they listen, it's of no avail
We all love our children, this is true
But does God listen to me and you?
Some problems he'll take and others make right
Will God listen to mankind's plight?
Man is a failure, this we all know
He showed us the way. Do we listen? *No!*

Carolee

AGGRESSION

Aggression! Progression! Regression! . . . a senseless act . . .
People of an unknowing, uncaring pact?
A sense of being noticed - of being known . . .
The idealisation of a boy who's fully grown.

Since a child, maybe he was left to drift - along life's open road
                                        of concord disharmony . . .
And then to shift still deeper - down a hill that's even steeper,
                                        to a chasm of senseless inequity.
Hooligans and vandals - individual people,
Like pathways to a church - with a grotesquely, gargoiled steeple.

The outside, one sees easily - and this is knowingly mocked . . .
But get to the heart and you get to the good - but the doors are
                                        mostly locked . . .
To find a key to fit the door to every situation . . .
Has proved one of life's complexities - with an ever-changing
                                        combination . . .

To fight the violence with violence - is like covering sand with sand . . .
Whilst with a little love and warmth and care - can make it fertile land.

Tony Armitage

HIS FLESH AND BLOOD

The vail of love which God once laid
As failed to stand the test
Man's troubled mind and angered thoughts
Brought to the world unrest
God set the world for all mankind
So say his chosen priest
Then why is it my world must be west
And their world must be east
The rules of life once carved in stone
By God's almighty hand
Now seem blinded from man's eye
And cast out like grains of sand
Love thy neighbour must stand true
Throughout our neighbourhood
Cast it wide across the world
We are all his flesh and blood
Spread the veil of love
Which God laid down
And treat it not unjust
Return to our Lord
The world He made
A world of love and trust

B Wardle

SEPTEMBER 11TH 2001

This fallen world, so civilised, developed,
Peopled by tribes intelligent, astute,
Outreaching forebears who dull with resignation
Laboured to graves forlorn and unremarked.
See how they sprang from caves, in skins,
Fighting their fellows club and knife, for status,
Burning antagonists, silencing dissent,
And never learnt.

They had their God: Jehovah, Allah, Christ,
And worshipped perfunctorily to measured statute,
Worshipped but listened not.
Dead to the God within.

See how they blossomed every other way:
To fly in planes heavier than air -
To live in towers a hundred storeys high -
To speak without wires.
    And to what end.
    Annihilation.
To fight better from the air,
To bury deeper from a tower,
To bid farewell by phone.

With nuclear power untapped, hell's last resort,
    Jehovah, Allah, Christ,
    Forgive our trespasses.

Joyce Barton

DARE WE HOPE?

Hearts filled with hatred, misguided pride,
each one believing right's on their side,
refusing to meet, talk with each other,
they'd sooner fight than call men 'brother'.

Political power that some men wield,
stubborn, determined they'll never yield.
Innocent victims, everyday folk,
see through the screen of government smoke!

Whatever nation or religion,
none prepared to make a decision.
The ugliest pictures fate now draws,
biological, chemical wars.

Torment, torture in many a land,
men, women, children don't understand
why their lives are filled with such pain,
why they were born seems pointless, in vain.

Inspite of it all, hope brings desire
that peace will come and put out the fire.
Despots, dictators, one day will die,
leaving the world fit for you and I.

Ann Odger

INGRATITUDE

Why did you fight for us, why did you die?
On the ground, in the sea and the sky
Such ingratitude reigns everywhere
For your sacrifices they don't care.

The would have loved the freedom we have now
Men don't trudge the furrows behind the plough
They have tractors to do the hard work
Hard work you did! You didn't shirk!

In the office they don't have too much
They have machines, computers and such
They don't need brains, just press a knob
And all the machines do their job.

When I think of your sacrifice my blood boils
Yours bled and you died, you got no spoils
And for your lives I say why did you die?
Why dear God will you please tell me why?

Not a day goes by but I think to say
Thank God for young men's bravery and I pray.
Thank God for my freedom, for my life free from strife
For the freedom You carried for me and made with your life

Marjorie Wagg

IN TROUBLED TIMES 2001

Men in battles, men in war
Fighting for country, fighting to
Score a hit, against their opponents,
Against terrorism.
Fields with blood soaked grass,
Men in fear for their lives.
A duty that has to be done, by soldiers
Men waiting in silence for the first
Sound of gun, who will be the first to shoot.
Trench is their refuge
Will it be their grave?
A battered photograph, pictured thoughts
Of those back home,
Might be memories for some,
For others their tomb.
Let there be peace, let peace prevail
Save the innocent, especially the children
And women. Let there be peace, Let
Them survive. These troubled times.

Jean Nicholls

NEW BEGINNING
(Dedicated to inmates of H M Prisons)

It is difficult for many of us
'Because of our states of mind'
To welcome a new year . . .
With a truly open heart
When it will bring upon us more
. . . Expectations to overcome

Longing, is our main thought
For everything beyond these walls
Mixed with bitterness for the system
And blaming everyone else for our faults
. . . I wish it could be repentance!
So we won't come back any more

We should rejoice from today!
Though we are social outcasts
'Cos not everything is lost
For the future is still to come
Giving us time to put it right
Reflecting on all we have done

We often think out loud . . .
Nothing is worse than this confinement!
Though we are free of responsibilities
Which others have now taken in charge
. . . Like the loved ones we have left
To make it in the world without us

Remember when we used to have
The best of wishes for their lives?
What has happened since then!
Let's put our rancour aside
There isn't much, which they can do
. . . They need us badly by their side

Let's pull them out of their pits
... That we have so deeply dug
Let's make amends right now!
Now, that we still have some time

Let's not make worse our future
With our egotistical ways
letting our children succumb
'Cos we showed them nothing else
Let's make them feel proud ...
That we have tamed our past

Forget about all the excuses!
On our deeds we must reflect
For our families well being
That have trusted our manhood leaves

Let's now make peace with society
... Through our learnings inside
I assure you we have lots to offer
They'll be pleased to share with us
... 'So Cheers!'
For this bright and new opportunity
To be needed! ... as we need their trust back

This is my message to us ...
Fellow mates in times of trouble
Hoping my words haven't hurt you
But make some sense in our exile
'Cos I feel your pain my friends
... Which gives understanding to mine

So welcome the years ahead!
Walking with God side by side
Not forgetting this experience
That has brought us close together
... 'For the benefit of our lives'

Eduardo Del-Rio Escalona

HOW MANY DID YOU SAY?

How many did they say, in America, have been blown away?
What an awful price to pay, but for what?
For being innocent is it not?
Islam, what is that to do with it?
The terrorists, do they not just use it?
It seems to me they more abuse it, sad to say
For where in whatever religion there be
Does such cruelty exist, is war, just some melee?
A chance to be noticed, or is it really poverty, is behind it? I wonder
Innocent lives are being lost daily, even in Afghanistan,
And I don't mean maybe
Kabul is half empty, more refugees aplenty
Babies, children, mothers, heartbroken too
And many may ask, I have no doubt
Where is God, where is salvation found, to be true?
If the Americans were supporting Palestine say
Instead of Israel, I ask you, today, what then world tell me do
Is war, not human madness, is war not grief and sadness,
Being allowed, but here, to win through, man, stop
And think again, please do, let God in, let Christ get through to you
Christian or Jewish, is it alone, is the enemy?
And not the sin in you and I, that truly God cannot
Condone? No lie! As that one weakness in sinner
You and I, is the reason alone, we do die,
Osama Bin Laden does not give a damn either - forbye

M Lightbody

MORE THAN A WAISTCOAT

Beneath bitter Bowler,
beneath the sash,
beneath the Queen's Highway,
pounded by so many parading boots,
beneath the kerbs painted red, white and blue,
Ulster is so much more than a waistcoat
covering tainted hearts;
it is an ancient nine-country province,
where once dwelt Ireland's High Kings.

Perry McDaid

THE LAST WORD

If, just once, you'd stop and let me finish what I'm -
You'd realise, this once, that there's no bloody point in -
I've phoned a cab. Here - take my keys. You know that I'm not -
In a week or so, I'll have my lawyer phone, or contact you in -
Of course I'm filing for -

Because I can't take any -
I'm sick of fighting, tired trying, and now I want it -
All we do is count each other's faults. Well, I'm fed up keeping -
What love we may have had is dying and it's not going to -

I know how cruel I seem, but I can't do this and be -
You can't stop me walking out of here, no matter what you -
You can shout me down, cut me off: It's not going to change my -
I'm leaving you. Whether or not you hear me say -
goodbye.

Damien Kelly

HOMELESS

Surrogate Mother
Sperm donor dad
I am a freak of nature
A designer fad

An Armani nose
Calvin Klein eyes
Programmed brain-cells
Million dollar disguise

I was conceived in a test tube
Bought over the phone
I was not what they ordered
Left all alone

One little defect
It's only DNA
Not one hundred per cent to order
My owners refused to pay

Twenty-first century baby
Replica of an aborted clone
Used, soiled and discarded
I only want a home.

Andrew Ryan

ANGER

Brain steaming!
An upset of a kind,
An unfriendly word spoken!
Events of unfavoured,
In mind,
A collision of thoughts,
To stir wrath,
Within peace of mind,
An unpremeditated -
Flow of unfriendliness,
Callous -
Or cold hearted -
Flow of storm clouds,
Amid life,
Strewn with predicaments,
From calm - to storm,
Rages - feelings
To be misunderstood,
Within emotions -
Or caring,
A chance to lose steam
Upon the innocent,
Lest!
Such storm mellow
Within secluded minds,
To withdraw tamely,
From the anger.

Steve Kettlewell

A SIGN OF THE TIMES . . .

(Dedicated to all those anti-environmentalists, who like nothing better than 'acid' rain . . .)

Monday's child will suffer grief
Shooting up heroin, in search of relief . . .

Tuesday's child sells their body for cash
To earn enough money to buy some hash . . .

Wednesday's child will spew up their 'brekkie'
After a night spent swallowing 'eccy' . . .

Thursday's child has disfunctional brain
From snorting up all those lines of cocaine . . .

Friday's child drinks - thinking he's mellow
Till his liver packs in and his skin turns yellow . . .

Saturday's child looks calm and placid
Suspended in the limbo of 'dreamworld' acid . . .

And Sunday's child has succumbed to greed
He uses all six, along with some speed . . .

Enrico

BLUE

I watch them driving past,
Snot running from their large pink snouts.
When you come near,
They snuffle at you, grab at you,
Search you at gunpoint
And bundle you into their cars.
They take you back to the sty,
Offer you something from the trough
(Such hospitable animals);
Then they shoot questions at you,
Put words into your mouth,
Shout you down until you cry
And own up to things you never did.
They lock you up,
Snort and grunt at you
From little windows in the doors.
Then they let you go and
Leave you alone on the streets.

Away from the safety of the sty,
They no longer give a damn.
They go home and beat their wives,
Abhor the law and order,
And generally live like pigs.

Suie Nettle

I Only Came Here To Breathe

When I am born, I demand convenience in my life.
I demand to be breast-fed McDonald's milkshakes and Coca-Cola.
I want corporate logos tattooed onto my gentle young skin.
I will be a walking advertisement for ICI and Ford and Hollywood.
I want my first words to be 'commerce', and my first steps taken
in a mall.
I want to be praised as a God as I cast aside my litter to the concrete
hive in which I dwell, and my day to day fumes and aerosols and
poisonous wastes shall be counted as blessings to all.
I want the O-zone to open up above me like a halo, and the
ever-increasing oceans to take me in their cleansing waves.
Testing on animals will be my playful learning, and my shitty
teenage cashier jobs will be viewed as wonderful and inspiring.
The drugs that I will get into will be fuel that keeps me real,
and the soul that I will be crushing will be like me simply shedding
my skin.
My thoughts of happiness and positive relations will be replaced
with cynicism and contempt for all that does not provide what I need.
My demand for convenience will be my only passion. The relationships
that I have will be totally cold and wanton.
I will never have a good reason to be with someone and just their being
there will make me hate them with a natural, instinctive, territorial
paranoia that even this civilised society cannot escape.
I want my view of civilisation to be the only thing that keeps me free,
and I never want to see the computerised, clinical, mind-numbing
routines in my every day life for what they really are.
I want to smile and think that this is all I want to make me happy.
I want to carry on walking blindly until I die - never even coming close
to what I thought could make me truly happy.
I want my being ending up as a number on a form.
I want to be nothing more than a cog in the works.
Is this so much to ask?

Richard Fox

COWS IN COUNTY DURHAM

Foot and mouth
Ravaged through
Our countryside,
The footpath's closed
Wellington boots were hosed,
The warning signs went up!
People keep out!
Farmers stayed inside
Banished walkers, sighed,
Sadly burning fires were seen
In our fields of green,
The smoke smelled vile
Dark and dank, in the sky,
From farmers the shock
The tears, the grief, the mayhem,
All quietened for a while
Then suddenly they were seen
Cows, in County Durham.

Susan Carole Roberts

FARM HARM

The fronds there are waving - but nothing waves back,
As signs are appearing - stating 'stay off this track',
The fields they lie empty - no beast there in sight,
No chance of redeeming - though try as they might,
The farmers feel helpless - their planning awry,
Some have given up completely - to lay down to die,
Such drastic action - of course we must forgive,
No inspiration to continue - no encouragement to live,
Their flocks are now missing - it was not their fault,
Inspectors condemned their cattle - to succumb to a bolt,
Their numbers diminished - too sheep are not there,
A tragedy for this island - nothing like it to compare,
A hopeless situation - what a predicament they're in,
No income forthcoming - to provide for their kin,
A disease of great proportion - felt from the north to the south,
A disaster for our nation - is this damned *'foot and mouth'*,
so easy to catch - to pass on to a friend,
A disease that's so prevalent none can anticipate when it might end,
An illness compounded - by the transporting abroad,
An illness so infectious - taking away those adored,
Now empty those fields - nothing seen in the lanes,
An urgency is upon us - please rally the brains,
Of experts in chemistry - agriculture and such,
To at last save our country - because we love it so much,
Get a grip on this plague - help it eventually to cease,
Make it 'good riddance' forever - to this *bloody disease!*

John L Wright

DEFENCELESS LIVES

The life that burns,
And yearns to breathe.
One single day,
In blessed reprieve.
Of needles and liquids,
Which sting the skin
And the growing fear
That breeds within

To be free of tests
Which simply prove
That with each organ
That is removed
Life shall die
And never return
Yet with little result
And much to learn
They continue in vain
To violate
The life of animals
And without debate
They steal the hearts
Of defenceless lives
That they breed to bleed
In sacrifice.

Carla Marie Haynes

THE LAMENT OF THE SLAUGHTERED SHEEP

Phantom voices are heard in the wind at night
As it blows o'er the fells.
Plaintive the sounds borne faintly
They cry, 'Remember us and how we grazed
Happily, tranquilly on till foul disease
Forced man to kill us healthy as we were.
Now we lie buried in the land we loved,
Unsung by those in towns, who knew us not
But mourned by call of curlew, songs of birds.
Oh man, remember us in this sad year
And why we died.
Fight on against our enemy and yours
Till once again the fells are live
With springtime's lambs.
Your heritage, and ours.

Margaret B Baguley

SAVE THE POUND

The bureaucrats from Brussels
Want to take our rights away
They try to flex their muscles
And expect us to obey

First they changed the money
Followed by inches, feet and yards
We no longer think it's funny
'Cause more changes are on the cards

When Britons want to buy new cars
The Union Jack is banned
Number plates have Euro stars
Rules are getting out of hand

If you buy some fruit or veg
Weighed in Kilos, not in lbs.
The greengrocer must give his pledge
Or he's fined two thousand pounds

They changed the gallons to litres
We are ripped off to re-fuel
Soon, miles will be kilometres
Whether we travel by car or mule

Our sovereignty could be next in line
The choice is President or Queen
These rules from Europe we must decline
Or they may strip this country clean

Have we benefited from these changes?
Are we better off, or worse?
It's un-elected men, who re-arranges
Everything, that erodes our purse

Their bitter medicine we must sup
Dig those heels into the ground
The silent majority must speak up
If we're going to save the pound

Tom Rutherford

SEPTEMBER 11, AD 2001

Just another day
The same as before.
Just an aeroplane, flying over
The New York sky.

The aeroplanes take off
The disciples of terror
Lost in the faceless crowd
Time is approaching 8.56am.

I sit with my wife, watching the events
Is this real? Can it be? Could it be
The trailer of the latest horror fantasy?
Only Satan dare to write such an evil script.

An aeroplane collides
With the icon of New York pride
The crescendo of terror echoes
Smoke from the tower ascends.

The duet of terror, scream hell, rock and roll.
Could I be having a nightmare during daytime?
Falling cherry blossoms
Turning bloody-red, as they strike the pavement.

Two towering infernos.
Can you hear the screams
Echo inside my head?
Hate is the last religious sacrament.

Emergency, emergency,
To do their job, to save lives.
On the altar of humanity
In the line of duty they offer a living sacrifice.

Shaken to the core
By the furnace of hell
Jack-hammered by their weight
The twin icons crumble on their legs.

Winners or losers. Gambling
On a game of chance, for life.
Who shall never come home?
Who shall never knock on the door?

The ancient dream of the brotherhood of man.
Buried under the rubble of the New York sky
Infinite justice, to be politically correct?
A new holy war shall be declared!

A new chapter to ancient old history?
Collateral damage are women and children.
America, America. The avenger.
Hate is the last religious sacrament.

T Lawrence